READ THIS NOTE WHEN...

A COLLECTION OF SHORT, INSPIRATIONAL, AND UPLIFTING MESSAGES FOR TEEN GIRLS DURING EMOTIONAL MOMENTS

SHELLEY CARROLL

This book is dedicated to my beautiful daughter, Julia, who inspired me to write these notes as a guide for her and her friends during their teenage years.

CONTENTS

READ THIS NOTE NOW

The teen years, or adolescence, is the period in one's life that follows the onset of puberty, during which a young person transitions from childhood to adulthood. Adolescence is a challenging and fantastic chapter in your life, full of opportunity, growth, and sometimes hardships. It isn't always easy to navigate through some of the emotions, physical changes, and decisions facing you, and you may not always feel you have someone to turn to when dealing with them.

You have at your fingertips a series of messages designed for you to read when you experience certain emotions or when presented with challenges that arise during your young life. These notes are here to guide you, to reassure you, and to remind you that you're not alone. They aim to be uplifting, comforting, and empowering messages to refer back to as needed. Please read through all of them first, then return to a specific message when you need to elevate your mood, or you need advice.

Years ago, I created these notes for my daughter and her friends when they were young, and I want to share them with you.

May these notes make you smile and bring you solace, strength, and peace when you read them. May this time in your young life be filled with laughter, love, and harmony!

NOTE 1: READ THIS NOTE WHEN YOU HAVE HAD A GREAT DAY

It is time to rejoice! You have had a great day, and you must be feeling fantastic. Take a moment and absorb this feeling you have because of this wonderful day. Celebrate and be grateful for everything that has happened today to make this day great. Your gratitude for these positive experiences is a powerful force. Oftentimes, we spend more energy on and give more thought to the days that don't go our way than we do to the days that do. So take this opportunity to enjoy and remember everything about this day. Capture this day's joy in a journal, or write it down in the back of this book; it's a good keepsake for future reflections. Write about the events and how they made you feel, and write in detail what was special. When you write things down, they become more solidified in your memory. I want to bring to your attention that this is a perfect example of how things always get better, no matter how bad things seem or how bad things get. This great day proves it! When you feel sad or depressed or need a happy memory to bring up your mood, remember this day and the events that made it a great one. You are loved, and I rejoice with you on this wonderful day. May you have many more just like this one!

NOTE 2: READ THIS NOTE WHEN YOU ARE HAVING A BAD DAY

If you are reading this, you are either having a bad day or have had one. I am sorry you are having a rough day. You have been here before and most likely will be here again, but I hope these words will help you turn your day around and make it a better one.

First, I want you to take 10 very deep breaths. Inhale as deeply as you can, and exhale as deeply as possible. Oxygen to the brain is always a good place to start.

Now, nothing is going your way, right? Or has it been one disaster after another? If you perceive this day to be a "bad" day, know that the beauty of this day is that it will end, and tomorrow is another one. Tomorrow is another chance for it to be a great day, for you to make different decisions, and for good things to happen to you.

Remember that no matter how terrible it seems, it will get better. It always does. Just think about all the great days you have already had. You've overcome bad days before, and you can do it again. Try to take the "bad" out of this day by thinking happy thoughts, doing something you enjoy, and focusing on the present. Nothing dire is happening right this instant, so you have an opportunity right now to make this day better.

Also, and this is the most important thing, remember that not every moment of this day was bad. Think about all the things that have gone right today, and focus on those. Be grateful for those good times, and you will begin to see more of the "good" in your day, which will make the other less prominent. You are a wonderful person and are loved. Here's to a brighter tomorrow!

NOTE 3: READ THIS NOTE WHEN YOU ARE FEELING HAPPY

So you are feeling happy?! How wonderful! You deserve to be joyful and are worthy of happiness. Happiness is a fantastic feeling. Here is an opportunity to imprint this happy event into your memory and use this thought when you are sad.

Did you know it is impossible to be unhappy when thinking happy thoughts? Enjoy this feeling, remember this event that is causing you to feel happy, write it down, celebrate it, and return to this thought when you need it most. You may not be aware of this, but happiness is a choice. Life will bring you many challenges, and you have a choice in how you react to these challenges. You can choose to be happy and optimistic, or you can choose to be sad and pessimistic. The point is that the power of happiness lies within you. The more often you look for it, the more often it will appear in your life.

Happiness is also contagious, so share this experience with others! I am sure you have experienced this yourself. Remember when you were around someone happy? It is hard not to feel the same way, right? Hold onto this feeling as long as you can, and may you have many more happy times to remember!

NOTE 4: READ THIS NOTE WHEN YOU ARE FEELING SAD

I am sorry you are feeling sad. Let me start by saying it is okay to feel this way. Whatever the situation contributing to you feeling this way is, please know it will improve. It always does. For now, let's focus on thinking happier thoughts!

First, know you are loved, valued, and essential in many people's lives. Secondly, it is impossible to feel sad if you are thinking happy thoughts. What thoughts are you thinking right now? Let's change those thoughts into something that makes you happy. These thoughts may not change the situation, causing you to think sad thoughts, but they will help you feel better now.

Think of a memory, a scene in a movie, or anything that causes you to smile or laugh when you think about it. If you are having trouble coming up with something, here are some ideas: Is there a moment when your pet did something hilarious, or you saw a funny animal video? Remember when something funny happened to a sibling, friend, or even you? Think of a movie you love or parts you like that always make you smile. Think of a happy time or moment with the person you love. Think of trips you have gone on or places you have visited that make you smile.

Now, hold onto these thoughts for as long as you can. The longer you hold onto these thoughts, the more happy thoughts like this will come to you. Right now, thinking these happy thoughts, you should begin to feel better.

You can also engage in a task such as your favorite hobby, listen to uplifting music, or go for a walk to distract your mind. The task will elevate your mood as well and help distract you from your sadness. The key to making this effective is to immerse yourself in what you are doing. Concentrate and focus your energy on every aspect of what you are doing to distract yourself. If you feel like you are slipping into that sad state again, check your thoughts and change your sad thoughts into happier ones. Also, know that if an event has caused these sad thoughts, the effects of that event will fade in your memory and improve over time. Pain and sadness lessen over time; this is a fact, so keep this in mind.

Remember, when you are feeling sad, think happy thoughts! I have said this before because it is true: it is impossible to feel sad when thinking happy thoughts.

NOTE 5: READ THIS NOTE WHEN YOU ARE FEELING ANGRY

Anger is a powerful emotion. Being angry isn't necessarily a bad thing because it can provide clarity for necessary changes. However, it can lead to emotions that harm you both mentally and physically. When you are angry, you do not always think clearly, which can lead to behavior you might regret later. If this is one of those times, one of the best ways to change your mood is to take time out to compose yourself, do something productive, and think happier thoughts.

Positive thinking can help shift your focus from the source of your anger to more pleasant things, reducing the intensity of your emotions. Drink a glass of water. Then, take ten slow, deep breaths. As you inhale deeply, raise your shoulders to your ears and drop your shoulders down as you exhale. To take a deep breath properly, follow these steps:

- Exhale all of the air from your lungs.
- Inhale slowly and deeply through your nose, filling your entire lungs until you can't take in any more air.
- Slowly let the air out of your lungs through your mouth with your lips pursed like you are blowing out a candle.

The key to deep breathing is to do it slowly. To get the most benefit from deep breathing, do it 5-10 times. Engage in physical activities that will increase your circulation, like going for a short walk or bike ride, running in place for a few minutes, doing jumping jacks, or punching a pillow. These physical outlets can be powerful tools to help calm you down by releasing pent-up energy and reducing the physical symptoms of anger, so will be in a better frame of mind for making decisions about any action you might want to take.

If you are having trouble calming yourself, talk to someone close to you or reach out to someone you know can help calm you down. If no one is available to you now, your best action is to remove yourself from the situation and get involved in something else. Put this event aside for now and change your focus. You don't have to do anything about this situation right now. Try to change your thoughts to happy ones (see the note on "Read When You are Feeling Sad"). Total distraction is your ally right now.

Remember, you are loved and valued. This feeling is temporary; you have known peace before and will again. This situation will pass, and it will get better over time; it always does.

NOTE 6: READ THIS NOTE WHEN YOU ARE FEELING LONELY

Loneliness is a challenging emotion, often rooted in our perceptions of self. It is born from thoughts of low self-worth or feelings that you have no one close to you or do not deserve the closeness of others.

Maybe you feel lonely because it seems like everyone is in a relationship but you. Perhaps you feel detached from others because you cannot relate to the people around you. Maybe you think people do not like or love you for a specific reason. Believe me when I tell you that you are your worst critic. If you ask your friends and family these direct questions: "Do you love me?", "Am I worth being around?" or "Do you like me?" These people will emphatically tell you yes. You are worthy of friendship and love, and you bring uniqueness to this world. Close friendships and family relationships are significant to your emotional and physical health.

Think about what you are doing to be the best friend or relative to the ones you love. Is it the best you can give? If not, try reaching out to those closest to you and tell them how much they mean to you. Muster the courage to visit or call a close friend or relative and tell them how much you value them. I guarantee they will begin to tell you the same thing, and your relationships will improve and thrive.

If you feel that everyone has someone or is in a relationship, except for you, some words of comfort I can give you are that you are young and there are so many opportunities for relationships coming your way. This phrase may not help much, but keep it in mind and be excited about what is coming your way.

For now, make sure you are open to a relationship coming to you and not closed off. It isn't easy to approach someone who appears closed off, especially at this young age. Look around you - who do you see? Are you engaging with them? Try to focus on your close relationships with your friends. These friendships are essential and often suffer when you get busy or get into a romantic relationship because your attention may shift to the new love in your life. The other important people in your life often start feeling neglected.

You may feel lonely because you close yourself off to others due to being afraid of rejection or hurt feelings. Let me point out that no one can hurt your feelings without your permission. In other words, you can choose how you feel or react to what someone else says or does. You also have control over how you think. Rejection, in some form or another, is an inevitability in life. It is bound to happen. How you deal with it is up to you. Try not to take rejection personally. You are a wonderful and unique individual with much to offer others. If you get rejected by someone, it is not because of you as a person, although it is very easy to feel that way. Remember that you have a choice in how you think. You can feel hurt, sorrow, and anger at rejection, or you can lift your head, knowing it is not you person-ally, and move forward. Suppose you decide not to put yourself out there because of fear of rejection. In that case, you will likely miss many opportunities and possibilities to connect with others, which could lead to lifelong relationships.

You are never alone, even when you feel that way. Be patient and open for that new relationship to come your way because there are many opportunities for this throughout your life. Trust in the ones you love and the friends you have to be there for you. Believe in them, and they will believe in you. Be the person to your friends and family that you want them to be to you!

You have so much to offer others. You are inherently worthy, deserving of love, and capable of forming deep, lasting relationships! Keep your heart open and your spirit hopeful for the new connections that are on their way to you.

NOTE 7: READ THIS NOTE WHEN YOU ARE HURTING

If you are in pain, whether it be physical or emotional, one of the quickest ways to help alleviate the pain is to focus on something right at this moment that isn't hurting. Better yet, identify and acknowledge all the areas of your body where you feel good and are doing well. Pain in an area of your body can become all-consuming, and you can have difficulty concentrating on anything but the pain. If you take a moment to focus on and identify areas of your body that feel good right now, hold that focus as long as you can. By focusing on these areas, you can temporarily lessen the prominence of the pain.

Also, you can significantly alleviate physical pain by getting hydrated and increasing circulation. So, drink a tall glass of water, then try to do something to get your circulation going and your heart rate up. Go for a walk, ride a bike, do some stretching exercises for 15-20 minutes on all of the areas of your body that are not painful, and, if you can, try to do some gentle stretches on the sore area. Do what you can to increase your movement and circulation. Repeat this process throughout your day, and you should see an improvement in your comfort level.

If you are in emotional pain, the suggestions for relief are very similar:

- Distract your mind by focusing on all the promising areas of your life.
- Drink water to hydrate.
- Engage in stretching for 15-20 minutes.
- Take a walk or bike ride, and immerse yourself in your surroundings.

- Watch a funny movie or immerse yourself in
  an uplifting book.
- Listen to your favorite music.

Do anything to get your focus on something that makes you feel good, and you should see an improvement in your emotional comfort level.

Deep breathing is another essential tool to help reduce both physical and emotional pain. To take a deep breath properly, follow these steps:

- Exhale all of the air from your lungs.
- Inhale slowly and deeply through your nose,
  filling your entire lungs until you can't take
  in any more air.
- Slowly let the air out of your lungs through
  your mouth with your lips pursed like you
  are blowing out a candle.

The key to deep breathing is to do it slowly. To get the most benefit from deep breathing, do it several times a day.

Remember, you are loved and valued. This pain is temporary; you have had relief before and will again.

NOTE 8: READ THIS NOTE WHEN YOU FEEL BAD ABOUT YOURSELF

It is awful to feel bad about yourself. Maybe you're unhappy with your appearance and weight or feel like you've failed somehow. Any negative words you direct toward yourself can be destructive and hurtful; what benefit do you obtain from thinking this way? You are your worst critic. Think about the things you are saying about yourself right now. Would you say these things to your closest friend or family member? Most likely not; you probably wouldn't dream about saying these things to anyone you love. So, treat yourself with the same kindness you offer others. It's easy to forget how perfect you are. You bring a wonderful uniqueness to this world. Instead of harsh words, remind yourself of these truths:

- "I am beautiful."
- "I am worthwhile."
- "I am perfect right now."
- "I am worthy of everything good that comes to me."
- "I am a good person."
- "I am loved".

Now, focus on the things you love about yourself and say them out loud.

If you are feeling bad about a specific body part, shift your focus to the aspects of your body you love. If you are feeling like a failure, reflect on your successes. Instead of dwelling on poor choices, celebrate the good ones you've made and the fantastic things you have done and said.

Remember, you are beautiful, worthy, and loved. Embrace tomorrow as a new opportunity to feel better.

NOTE 9: READ THIS NOTE WHEN YOU ARE CONFUSED ABOUT WHO YOU ARE

This phase in your life can be incredibly tough and isolating. You're no longer a child, yet you might still feel that way inside. Others are making decisions for you because you're not yet an adult. It might seem like the expectations placed on you don't align with who you truly are. Your emotions are intense, and your hormones are in control.

Every adult has experienced this, and there is no magic recipe or a list of perfect steps to follow. No matter what's happening to you on the outside, remember that who you are, the "You" inside your body, is the perfect version of you now. Who you are inside will change over time as you mature, just like your body will change. You do not think or act the same as you did 5 years ago; in 5 years, you will not think or act the same as you do now. These years will be exciting, embarrassing, awkward, and magical. Most importantly, they will be short in the grand scheme of life.

So, if you are having a difficult time, don't worry, it gets better. If you are having a great time, store and cherish these memories so you can reflect on them later in life.

You are many things, not just one or two, and no rule says you have to be only one or two things. Feel free to enjoy as many roles or identities as you like, and allow yourself the freedom to change your mind at any time. Who you are is evolving and changing, so don't waste too much energy trying to figure out who you should be. Embrace and enjoy who you are now.

Because right now, you are, and at every point in the future, you will be, the perfect version of yourself!

NOTE 10: READ THIS NOTE
WHEN DECIDING ON A CAREER

It's that time in your life when you are being asked or told to decide what you want to do or be when you grow up and leave school. You may be in high school and preparing for college applications. Maybe you have decided not to attend college but are wondering what kind of job you will be able to get after you graduate from high school.

The university is not for everyone, which is perfectly fine. There are many wonderful ways to support yourself, and many critical jobs in society do not require a college degree. Regardless of your choice, you're feeling the pressure of making a decision now, or very soon, about what to do or be, which will affect the rest of your life! But remember, the power to choose is in your hands. So, let's calm down, take a few deep breaths, and get some perspective.

You might be hearing from your teachers, friends, parents, or guidance counselor (or from all of the above) that you must decide on your college degree path or declare a major now. They may tell you that college is challenging work or difficult to get into. They might be giving you statistics on how many people don't get in or don't finish college. This must be terrifying and incredibly stressful!

Well, as a college graduate, I'm here to tell you that it does not have to be that way. It doesn't have to be a scary process, nor is it imperative that you decide right now. If you're considering college, whether at a university or a community college, getting a course catalog and looking through it is a great idea. Go to a university or college campus nearby and take a tour. Talk to some students and instructors. If you don't know what career you are interested in, THAT'S OKAY. Investigate your options. Start looking for people in positions or jobs that interest you, who you can question or even shadow, to see if it truly is an area you would enjoy. The more information you have, the less scary this process will be.

If you must declare a major to apply to a university or community college and still don't know which one to choose, ask for guidance from someone you trust, then pick one and get started. This choice isn't set in stone, and you can always change your mind if you find out it wasn't the right choice.

If you can't attend college for whatever reason or don't want to, that's okay, too. You have been in school for a long time and may need a break from school. Believe it or not, you have many options if you are in high school or just graduating. The more flexible you are, the more options you'll have. Also, the more you look, the more you'll see. This idea may seem strange, but if you limit yourself to a certain kind of job instead of being open to what is out there and available, you may miss out on many opportunities.

Taking any job available to you right out of high school doesn't mean you'll have to do that for the rest of your life, but at least you can start making money immediately while figuring out what you want to do. Skilled labor professionals like electricians, masons, and plumbers are currently in high demand, and you can make a great living by providing a much-needed service. Best of all, you get paid while learning a skill.

Your teen years are an exciting time and a big step into adulthood. Please keep an open mind, make it an enjoyable process instead of a dreaded one, and then look for opportunities that will come your way! By keeping an open mind, you open yourself up to a world of possibilities and opportunities, making the journey into adulthood an exciting one.

NOTE 11: READ THIS NOTE WHEN HAVING RELATIONSHIP ISSUES

Relationships are complex because you are complex. Think of the roles and personality traits that make up who you are. You are a daughter, possibly a sister, a friend, or perhaps a girlfriend. You do not behave the same way toward each person in your relationships. How you act and interact with each person depends on your relationship, right?

You have complete control over how you choose to react, feel, and behave in any situation. Notice how I use the word choose? I use this word on purpose because you have a choice in everything. You have the power to decide how you react and communicate. Even when you choose not to make a decision, you're still making a choice. The sooner you grasp this fundamental aspect of life, the more manageable life becomes. The more you realize the control you have over your life and choices, the better equipped you'll be for whatever life throws at you.

Communication is the single most crucial aspect of any relationship. Consider this: you're not a mind reader; you can't read your mother's, friend's, or boyfriend's mind to know what they want or expect from you, right? And, neither can they.

Most people are not experts or even good at communicating. We have an idea we want to express, and we say it, write it, or text it without much thought about how we deliver our message. Problems arise when what we say, text, or write doesn't come across as we mean. In other words, we don't always convey our meaning effectively. Ineffective communication can and often does lead to misunderstandings. This is particularly true for written communication, where no body language or tone guides the interpretation of your meaning.

While there are numerous books on effective communication, the essence of it can be distilled into a few key principles. Mastering these principles can significantly enhance your communication skills, reduce misunderstandings, and foster healthier relationships.

1. When you speak to the person instead of texting or writing what you want to say, there are far fewer opportunities for misunderstanding. When you have something important to convey to the other person, talk to them.

2. After the discussion, if you feel you've effectively communicated your point, ask them what they heard you say or if they understood your meaning. Oftentimes, what you said or meant to say is not what they heard. What you meant to communicate wasn't received in the way you intended. Unintended meaning can be enormous and is likely the cause of most misunderstandings leading to relationship problems.

3. It's very common to believe there's a different meaning behind the words someone said to you. For example, you might think, "Well, he or she said this, but what they really mean is that." My advice is, don't do this! If you believe the person meant something different than what was said, ask them for clarification.

Finally, in a romantic relationship, expecting your partner to read your mind is neither realistic nor fair. You are setting yourself up for disappointment. We do not live in a rom-com or a romantic novel. It's not fair to your companion for you to expect this, and it will lead to relationship problems. Be clear about what you desire, hope, and want from them. Allow them to be spontaneous with when and how they give you these things.

Respect is the second most important aspect of any relationship. Respect is crucial. It means loving someone regardless of their views, and it encourages open expression without fear of judgment. When having a disagreement or argument, you show respect by acknowledging their ideas or feelings are valid, even though you may disagree. Agreeing to disagree is respectful. Self-respect also plays a key role; when you respect yourself, you're more likely to respect others.

Most relationship issues center around these two concepts, and if you develop effective communication skills and demonstrate respect, your relationships will begin to improve.

NOTE 12: READ THIS NOTE WHEN SOMEONE IS ASKING FOR HELP

Someone is turning to you for help, which means they trust you and feel safe asking for your help. Asking for help isn't always easy for people, and it might be difficult for you, too.

Keep in mind that just because they ask for help does not mean you must take care of them or act on their behalf, even though they might be asking this of you.

First, decide if you are in a position, either emotionally or physically, to act on their request for help. Or, will their asking for help put you in a difficult position that you don't feel is right for you?

If you decide you can and want to help, you might share your "Read This Note When" book with them. If the book helped you, it might help others, too. Helping another person can mean being available to be with them, supporting them, and listening to what they say. Being present and available to be there or listen is a valuable gift and can work wonders for someone. It might just be the exact help they need to help themselves.

Remember, you're not responsible for anyone else or their feelings. Still, you can benefit someone by offering your support, trust, encouragement, and belief in them and their abilities to overcome obstacles.

Be careful about promising to keep secrets; it might put you in a difficult situation, or keeping a secret may be more harmful to them. Trust your instincts and get help for the person if you feel they're in trouble.

Remind them they're not alone, they're worthwhile, and things will work out. Also, remind them that this situation will improve in time, as it always does!

ABOUT DEPRESSION

I don't have a section specifically addressing this topic because it's incredibly varied and complex. Most people with depression experience emotions in one or more of the areas I've discussed, so I encourage you to read over those notes that pertain to you that might be contributing to depression.

I will say if you're experiencing symptoms of depression, please reach out to someone for help.

Talk to your parents or guardians if you're able to. If you can't talk to them, reach out to your school guidance counselor, teacher, school nurse, or family doctor. If you belong to a church or religious organization, reach out to people you trust. They'll help you get the guidance and support you need.

If you don't belong to a church or religious organization, you can go to just about any church for help, even if you're not a member or a believer. If you're in a bad place mentally, you can walk into any emergency room, fire department, or police station for immediate help.

There are many tools and people available to you that can help you get through this. You are loved and valued.

You can dial 988 on the phone or go to this website https://www.samhsa.gov/mental-health/988 to reach the Suicide and Crisis Lifeline.

I want these notes to be a ray of hope, bringing smiles and moments of solace, strength, and peace into your life. Each message is here for you to revisit whenever you find yourself riding the currents of emotion, seeking a quick burst of encouragement, or simply needing a reminder of your inner strength.

Cherish this beautiful and fleeting time in your young life. Create memories you'll treasure for the happiness they bring and a guide you can turn to in times of need.

May your life be filled with laughter, love, and harmony.

Remember, every day is an opportunity to heal, grow, and celebrate the journey of being uniquely you. Embrace each moment, and may you find the strength to face any challenge and the courage to live life to its fullest.

Please share this book with your friends and family if you found it helpful. They may also find it useful.

I would greatly appreciate it if you left a favorable review of this book on the site where you purchased it.

Happy Thoughts and Events to Remember

Use this section to write down a few happy moments and good thoughts to help you during sad or bad days.

www.ingramcontent.com/pod-product-compliance
Lightning Source LLC
Chambersburg PA
CBHW061640130726
47996CB00003B/1383